Finishing
Touches

Edited by Gregory E. Buford

DEDICATION

This book is dedicated to the authors' friends and families—past, present and future.

CONTENTS

ACKNOWLEDGMENTS

The authors wish to acknowledge the support of Cynthia A. Alexander, who encouraged them to write their stories, Thrivent Financial, Sergio and Judi Amaya, Wildflower Terrace and Gregory E. Buford.

1 A LOVELY LITTLE ITALIAN LADY
Martha A. Obergfell Downing

My grandmother Agusta Bianchi came to the USA in the early 1800's from northern Italy. (She always said northern Italy was better than southern Italy.) She settled in the mining town of Ouray, Colorado, with her husband Lawrence Tessiatore. She was a mail-order bride.

Nona cooked for the miners, Mr. Tessiatore, and two other men who died of miner's consumption. She had three children with Mr. Tessiatore—Lawrence, Tony and my mother, Margarite. Nona had a series of apartments which rented to miners after her husband died. She was a tiny woman—less than five feet tall. She disliked wearing coats and so wore layers of dresses to keep warm.

Nona's children were successful. Tony owned a fruit farm in Grand Junction, Colorado. My mother earned a teaching degree in 1923 and married my father, who owned a ranch in Roubideau, Colorado. Lawrence made a living traveling all over Colorado repairing things for people.

When my grandmother visited us on the ranch she liked to drink the yolk of an egg from the shell. She had beautiful long hair which she wore in a bun. She lived in Ouray until her death.

2 MY BEDTIME PRAYER
Dr. Barbara Manroe

When I was three, I had a framed picture of a young girl praying on her knees. She had braided hair, and her eyes were closed. I thought she was named "LayMe" and that she was an angel.

My mother taught me to say a prayer every night before I went to bed. It made me feel very sleepy.

> *Now I lay me down to sleep*
> *I pray the Lord my soul to keep*
> *If I should die before I wake*
> *I pray the Lord my soul to take*

Because I was three years old, I could not read. I thought the "I lay me" part of the prayer meant the angel's name was LayMe. I can still see her in my mind even though I am seventy-four years old. She and God have kept me safe through times when the doctors told my family I was going to die. Indeed, I was very sick for a long time, but I did not die.

I have been very sick some more, but evidently it is not yet part of God's plan for me to die just yet. LayMe is still a part of my nighttime   prayers.

3 REMEMBRANCES
Leora "Mickey" Bishop

Mom

Mom was doubtless the strongest influence on my life as I was growing up, and that influence continues to affect my choices, beliefs and attitudes. I'm the youngest of her four children and the only one that lived with her full-time until I left home for college. Mom was a firm believer in education. She saw it as the ticket to a better life and let the four of us know we were expected to go to college. Only God knew how we were going to do that, but, somehow, all four of us made it.

When mom and Finace—the man I think of as my father—got together in Denver they built a two story house. While they built it we lived in a tent on a wood platform. My brother Harley stayed with Mom, Finace and me, and Sam and Patti lived with Dad, all of us in Denver at that time. That tent wasn't the easiest living quarter, and soon the four of us rented a basement house. We had to go down stairs to get to the basement, and there were some windows that let in a little light. Meanwhile, construction continued on our home. It was beautiful, white and elegant. I was looking forward to living in it, but, for some reason I didn't understand, it was sold. I was pretty young, and my memory of that time is quite fuzzy.

After the house sold, Finace and Mom bought a sawmill in the mountains. The closest town was Toponas, and we drove our logging truck into town only when it was absolutely necessary. Toponas was a small, close-knit community, and we were not welcome. Sometimes we went on through Toponas to Yampa. Yampa was bigger and much more welcoming.

The sawmill rested in a beautiful valley. Log cabins stood in a curvy line along the rippling creek that flowed down from the mountain. The cabins weren't particularly well built, likely intended for summer use only. The sturdiest one became our new home. Mom scrubbed the wood plank floors with lye. After rigorous cleaning and many repairs we moved in.

The cabin had a living room and single bedroom. We found a cast-iron stove in a pasture and made it our heat- and cook-stove. The stove had four burners, a water well and a big oven. Mom did a lot of baking and had to prop the oven door closed with a stick. Homemade curtains covered the windows. I think there were only two or three windows, but I'm certain we had no running water or electricity. A window box kept perishables in the winter, and in the summer we kept a food box in the creek. The outhouse was across the creek and, boy, was that snowmelt creek cold! Big, thick Montgomery Ward or Sears catalogs were our toilet paper. To this day, I'm very fussy about toilet paper.

Mom loved flowers, so in the summer we built a flower bed of logs and filled it with rich soil from the cow pasture. The flower bed held a colorful array of flowers: blue and white Columbines, yellow and purple daisies, lupine, sunflowers, and pink wild roses, to name a few. Mom poked holes in the bottom of an empty Folgers can with an ice pick, filled the can with horse manure and water from the creek and spread that over her flowers. She glowed with pleasure whenever she saw flowers coming into full bloom and when she received compliments on the beautiful display. That flower bed gave all of us a lift and brought happy smiles even on less than wonderful days.

Mother home-schooled Harley and me in the winter. In the mornings we did lessons, and in the afternoons the three of us went sledding on the mountain. So much fun! We looked forward to winter, because Mom wasn't so involved in the running of the mill and the skidding of the logs with the horses. She was much more relaxed and happy in winter.

Where Did *You Get That Name?*
I have two older brothers and an older sister. My sister's name is

Patricia, and we called her Pat or Patti. In those days, off-color Pat, Mike and Mustard jokes were popular. So when I was born my dad got excited and said, "We'll name her Mike."

Grandma Percy said, "You can't call a girl Mike."

"Okay then," he said. "We'll call her Mickey."

My given name is Leora Lorraine after my mother and great-grandmother, but "Mickey" stuck, except for formal or legal situations. I'm sure glad they didn't name me after Mustard, the prankster. I can't imagine being called Mustard!

My Father

My father joined the navy on April 17, 1944 when I was three years old. He served active duty on a supply ship, the USS Arequipa, in the Pacific. He mustered out on March 31, 1945, when I was four years old. I have no clear memory of him until Mom and I went to meet him when he returned from the war.

Mom seemed excited. She wore her prettiest dress, fussed with her hair and twirled around and around in front of a mirror checking out how she looked. I remember walking through a field—brown dirt, dead grass and weeds—on a crisp cool day to meet him. The sun was shining, producing a little warmth. My parents spied each other and met with warm hugs and kisses, their joy obvious and exciting. I was a little behind Mom. Finally they broke apart and Dad saw me.

"Ah, is this my Pat," he asked with a gleam in his eye.

"No, this is Mickey," Mom replied

"Oh," he said, visibly let down.

He took Mom's hand and started walking home. My sister, his girl, was actually named after one of his old girlfriends. He had no time for me ever. I think that was the start of me learning to stay in the background and not be noticed.

My next clear memory of him was when the three of us—Mom, Dad and me—were in a clearing, probably in our backyard. It was cloudy, and Mom and Dad were yelling and screaming at each other. Mom was crying. Dad began to hit her as they cursed each other, and I started kicking and hitting him. He grabbed me and shook me. "Stop it," he yelled, "or you're next!" I don't know what stopped the fight. Maybe the cops or the neighbors came.

Mom had a friend named Corky, a very large but loving woman, who gathered us kids up and took us to her house. Mom must have been taken to the hospital. She joined us later that night. Her face was bruised and swollen, and her eyes were black and blue. She had cracked ribs wrapped with a large bandage. We kids were scared and huddled together, trying not to cry or make a fuss

Later—I'm not sure how long—they divorced. Mom got custody of Harley, my oldest brother, and me. Dad got custody of Sam and Patti, the two middle kids. A few years ago I talked to Harley about it. He said the judge interviewed him and asked him who he wanted to live with. Harley said he told the judge that if he had to live with Dad he would find a way to kill the son of a bitch. I've never talked to Sam or Patti about it. I think it was odd that Dad got custody of any of us. Harley said he thought it was probably because Dad was returning from the war and was given special consideration. Mom never talked about it.

I divorced at twenty-nine and had two babies to raise. I dated, but if any relationship started looking serious I said, "You may work me or my kids over once, but never twice." I think this was a consequence of seeing my dad beating up my mom. I thank God that never became to an issue for me.

As time has passed I've mulled it over and learned important lessons. I believe it's important to practice compassion and forgiveness. It's taken years, but, after much thought and many prayers, I realize Dad lived a violent life, appeared to have no positive role models and eventually learned to control his anger and violence. It was my mother's place to forgive him, and I think she did. Who am I to judge?

My Father Figure

The man I think of as my father is Finace. He came into our lives when I was four or five. He was stocky but surprisingly limber. He had gunmetal gray hair and gray eyes and wore khakis that mom washed, starched and ironed. Khakis were his work uniform and his daily wear. Finace worked in road construction, and when he came home in the evening he was covered with dirt and sweat. The only thing clean was the area around his eyes, because he wore goggles on the job.

Finace was fifteen years older than Mom, and it was obvious he loved her. He used to sing to her with a big smile on his face—"You are my sunshine, my only sunshine. You make me happy when skies are gray." Mom wasn't always easy to get along with, but Finace tried hard to please her, often without much success.

Finace was an adventurer and frequently gone for two years at a time working on air bases in what was then French Morocco. He had worked on the expansion of the Panama Canal and suffered bouts of yellow fever. He had worked on the Yukon Highway and showed us pictures of the cook feeding a black bear club. Finace liked to tell jokes and had played minor league baseball. He watched the baseball games at every opportunity after we moved to Southern California and got a TV.

Finace also loved me. Mom always packed for him a black metal lunch box with a Thermos in the lid. She usually included a dessert, and he saved part of it for me. When he came in from work he would hand me his lunch box, and there would be a cupcake, cookie or some kind of treat.

Finace loved airplanes, and, if there was a barnstorm within driving distance on his day off, we would go. The daring of the stunt pilots and wing walkers took my breath away. We never took any rides, but the shows were astounding and stimulated my imagination. When we moved to Southern California, Finance took us to Los Angeles International Airport for a special treat on an occasional Sunday. We would go up on the flight deck and watch the planes land and take-off. I liked all the planes, but especially Trans World Airlines and Pan American because they flew to exotic places all over the world. After we had enough of watching planes we would go to the airport restaurant for lunch.

Another of Finace's joys was round track car racing. This kind of racing, like the barnstorming fly-ins, took place mostly in rural areas in Kansas and around Victorville or China Lake in California. We would check out the cars before the race and make bets with each other. Whoever won would get a banana split or an ice cream sundae. Finace introduced us to many activities and fun outings. I still go to air shows whenever the opportunity arises, and I still enjoy people-watching in airports. I even worked at the downtown Kansas City Airport in the 1960s and was a passenger service agent for Frontier Airlines. Attending car races was a big part of my life for many years, though not much anymore.

In August of 1957, Mom, Finace and I were preparing to go to what was then Siam. Finace had work there, and, finally, we would get to go with him. He had passed the required physical, and our excitement was mounting. I was in Northern California at that time helping my sister; she had just had her first son in July. Then I got a call. I needed to get home immediately. Finace had died of a stroke. He was 59 years old. I was 16. To say I was devastated doesn't begin to describe the depth of my sorrow.

Grandmother

At the end of first grade there was trouble. Someone was trying to take over the sawmill, and Mom and Finace were trying to hold on. Shots were fired. It got scary and ugly. Harley and I were sent to live with grandmother in Ignacio, Colorado. Harley stayed there for a while and then went to live with Uncle Edwin and Aunt Iris on their farm. They had six kids of their own. Our cousin Floyd was about the same age as Harley, and maybe it was nice for him to have another helping hand.

Grandmother was about five feet and four inches tall and never overweight. She was tough as nails and always wore dresses. She lived in a small rental house and worked in the local drugstore. She always had a cow, a Guernsey or a Jersey because they gave the richest milk. She scoffed at Holsteins. Grandmother milked the cow twice a day and sold most of the milk after separating the rich cream. I went with her to milk the cow. That cow didn't like me, and I was afraid of her since the time I climbed into the corral and she chased me around, lifted me with her horns and threw me over the railing. I like seeing cows and cattle in pastures, but I keep my distance.

Grandmother also butchered chickens, chopping off their heads on a chopping block and removing all the feathers and feet and such. When the chickens were cleaned up and care had been taken to remove all the pin feathers, they were dipped into a hot, yellow wax to preserve them and stored in a rented box at the local food locker.

Grandma was married five times. Her first husband and child tried cross a river in a heavy rainstorm on horseback. They were swept away by the strong current and died. After that she was terrified of rivers and especially the ocean. Her second husband was Mother and Uncle Edwin's father, Alonzo C. They were divorced. Her third husband was Denver L. He was a rancher—and a hell raiser when he went to town and got drunk. Grandma was a farmer, and the two collided. Mother adored him until he killed her pet pig in a drunken rage. Husband number four was Doll F. Were instructed to call him Uncle Doll. I never understood that. Husband number five was Grandma's childhood sweetheart, Grandpa Petersen. We all loved and adored him. He had been a shepherd for the Southern Ute Indian tribe. He always had a well-trained sheep dog, and watching Grandpa and his dog work sheep was a marvel.

Divorce was not acceptable back then, and one of the ways grandmother supported herself between husbands was by breaking horses. She had a hard time taking care of Uncle Edwin and Mom, so they were often farmed out to various relatives. Mom mostly stayed with relatives on her father's side of the family rather than with any of Grandma's relatives. Her father was an outcast; I think it was because he was a nonviolent, Seventh Day Adventist vegetarian in a cattle-raising family. Her father's family was a wild bunch with a bad reputation that followed them for years in Southern Colorado.

Later in life after Grandpa Peterson died, Grandma lived with my cousin, Doris, and her family. She died at the age of eighty-nine and was buried in the cemetery in Pagosa Springs, Colorado.

A New Chapter

I recently decided I wanted to be closer to my family, partly because my daughter and her husband adopted a baby. This blessing came out of the blue, surprising and thrilling us all. Brooklyn was born December 11, 2016. Such a Joy!

I lived in New Mexico. My daughter, Erica, had lived in Austin, Texas, over twenty years and my son, Tom, and his wife lived on a ranch outside of Granbury. I had been feeling a need to be more involved with my children and their families, and with the arrival of Brooklyn the desire became much stronger. Erica said, "Oh, Mom. We need to get you out here." She did some research online, checking out over a hundred options, and decided Wildflower Terrace would be the best choice. After careful consideration and many phone calls we decided to go forward. Paperwork was sent, corrected, and sent again. It was like nothing I'd been through in my seventy-eight years. Finally Jean from the Wildflower office called to say I had an apartment on the third floor. Yeah!

We were told we could move in on Fridays, so we rearranged our plans to accommodate. We arrived on a Friday morning ready to pay the deposit and rent, sign the lease, and start moving. We were told we couldn't do that until 2:00 PM because someone named Brenda had to do some paperwork first, and she'd taken the day off on Thursday. After some heated discussion we were told to come back at noon. I was thinking, "What have I gotten myself into?"

When we returned at noon all was much calmer. Brenda and I went over twenty-plus pages of the lease with me initialing and signing as quickly as I could. I got the keys and a "fob." What in the world was a fob? I didn't know, but Brenda make it clear an extra one would cost $250. My son-in-law and his workers began unloading the truck and trailer. My new apartment was jam-packed. I spent two nights at my daughter's until my bed was put together and we made a trip to the grocery store.

I thought I would have a sun room, but instead I have a balcony—a big plus. There's a "killer view," as my family says, of the Austin skyline. "A great place to watch the 4th of July fireworks!" I love it! I enjoy seeing the sunrises and the colorful sunsets. On the night of the full moon the view is stunning, and the next morning the moon is still up. Then the sun rises, casting a golden aura over downtown. What a blessing!

There's a lot going on at Wildflower Terrace. Resident and company calendars are in the information packet. Time to come out of hermit mode, but I want to get some kind of order in the apartment first. Filled boxes stuff the place. I take a break to attend an ice cream social sponsored by the Canasta Club. Three lovely ladies are seated at a table. I ask if I may join them. They smile and welcome me. Later Betty H. from the Wildflower office puts a tenants' directory under my door with a note saying to call her if I need anything. So thoughtful. The friendliness and kindness of the residents is already making a positive impact on my decision to start a new chapter. There's so much to be grateful for:

- A laundromat on every floor
- Warmth and kindness of the residents
- The elevator
- Decorations in the common area
- Carpet in the bedroom and a short hallway
- Ceiling fans and air conditioning
- Blinds on the windows and balcony doors

- Cynthia's literary salon
- Sharon P. taking me on a tour of the building and showing me how to get to the courtyard
- So many activities to pick and choose from

Thank you all! My new chapter is off to a great start!

4 GIGI
Paula Alvelo

Gigi—that's me—gets more emotional about good-byes than normal people do. I've had too many of them. By the time I was 10 years old, I'd already moved six times and been to three schools.

In fifth grade my best friend's name was Janet. She had curly hair, a fun giggle and a love for dill pickles. There was no hot lunch program, so Janet and I shared the sandwiches we packed from home. When I could, I brought extra pickles for her.

About six weeks after school started, my dad came home from work one evening and told us we were moving to a town ninety miles away. The next morning he took me to school, walked me into my classroom and told my teacher I was leaving.

The kids got quiet and stared at me as I cleaned out my desk. I wasn't allowed to say good-bye. I can still see Janet's face at the back of the room. She was crying silently, like I was. By that afternoon I was at a new school.

The same thing happened another six times before I graduated high school. I had quit making good friends because it didn't seem worth the trouble. Since then, I've learned that good friends are worth everything.

5 MY GREAT-GRANDMOTHER
Gilda Drew Mather

My great-grandmother Sarah Elizabeth Tanner Shaw, was a pioneer-type woman. She was sixteen when Abraham Lincoln was president. She used to wear a bonnet and an apron over her dress. There was a pocket on the apron where she kept her little corncob pipe. She always puffed on that pipe. (I'm unsure whether she inhaled or not!) She was at least half Native American Indian. The tribes we don't know. Some say Cherokee, some say different things, but she lived in a little village called Wahee Neck in Marion County, South Carolina. She had a place in the woods near fields and a river. She walked everywhere she went.

Back to her smoking. Everyone told her smoking was a sin. She prayed about it on her knees. She said, "Lord, if smoking is a sin, let the taste be bitter in my mouth. Then she got off her knees and puffed on her little pipe. She said, "It was the sweetest I've ever tasted."

Sarah's husband, Baker Shaw, was a Confederate soldier and was wounded in the Civil War. During this time my great grandmother was eight months "with child" as they would say. When the war was over Baker walked barefoot all the way from Virginia to South Carolina. He got home with bleeding feet and soon died of something.

So my great-grandmother was left a widow with eight children, all girls accept my grandfather, Leon Frank Shaw. They called my grandfather "Tom." I don't know why he was called Tom, but he was

13

the only boy in their family. When my Great-Aunt Baker was born, my great-grandmother would put her in a basket and leave her at the end of the row as she picked cotton. She'd check on her going up and down the rows of cotton, picking cotton for 40¢ a day.

My great-grandmother was a good, God-fearing woman who knew the Bible, though she could not read. She loved the Good Lord Jesus and depended on Him for everything. She was a praying woman throughout her life. All the storms of life, she weathered them all. My mother, Louise, would read her grandmother the Bible. She also taught me and my sister and brother. There are many true stories passed down through my mother, my aunts and great-aunts that are very worth telling. I hope to put those in a book of my own one day soon.

Sarah Elizabeth lived to be 103. The doctor said her body just gave out. She had no saliva in her throat and couldn't live because of that. She is someone I would like to see and hug and talk to if I could. I'm hoping to go to Heaven one day for I will know her when I see her, and she will know me, too. There's much more to Sarah's story. Her first two children, Della and Doug, died young. Della was twelve when she died; Doug was only four.

6 My ABC's
Leora "Mickey" Bishop

These are the ABC's I would like to impact my life:

- Adroitness, so I could paint my bedroom walls instead of calling in handyman Dave.
- Banter between us as Dave rolls on the Soft Fawn and Alabaster White trim.
- Charisma oozes off Dave, a stocky perfectionist.
- Diligence to complete a task used to be part of me, and I wish it would return.
- Experience. Maybe I could use less of that.
- Flexibility of movement seems to be part of who Dave is.
- Graceful movements and interaction, once so natural to me, have diminished.
- Happiness would reign if more of it returned.
- Imagination would make my writing so much easier.
- Joy is stylish jeans with elastic in the waistband.
- Kindness on a national scale would be a welcome relief.
- Love is the bottom line where we could all flourish.
- Money may not buy happiness, but more of it would ease stress.
- Naps, ah yes, I unapologetically take one when I need it.
- Options open doors.
- Perspectives which increase the...
- Quality of my life.
- Reggae music lets me...
- Sway and swing and relax.

- Time with my family.
- Unity, harmony and peace gained through…
- Visions of what could be and…
- eXcitement, breaking from the doldrums.
- Yin and yang to balance mind and body and put more…
- Zip in my step.

7 THINGS TO PONDER
Cynthia A. Alexander

A Visit

I lay here thinking! Worrying is what it's really called. My heart hurts for lack of things I care not to mention in so many people's lives. I stressed over it until I saw the dove on the window screen. His eyes were the most beautiful pink I had ever seen. His body the whitest white. Then the voice said, "Everything is going to be alright."

Lost

I knew one day I would be alone. I knew my immediate family would be gone before me. How I knew it I do not know. In Dallas Texas as a young woman, I imagined what it would be like to continue living without the people I loved so much. I wanted to feel it before it became real. I never wanted to be alone—but here I am with my mother, father, grandmother, grandfather, sister, brothers, nieces gone. Wow!

But You Can't See Him

How many times do we talk on the phone without seeing the person? Hear about someone who would be great for you? Imagine what it would be like on that new job you've been promised—and never see that person responsible for that news.

So you don't believe in God? We don't see Him either. It's ok if you don't believe—it's ok. One day we will see the person we're talking to long-distance. One day we will see the person someone

17

said would be great for us. One day we will be working on that new job we were promised. We will see that person responsible for that news.

I Noticed Something Was Wrong

It is January 1996. Curtis is having a good day. Curtis is my brother. We're doing lots of things together—and that makes him happy. Before Curtis came to live with me, he lived with my cousin Charles in Dallas. Charles called one day to say I needed to come get Curtis because he had sold Nana's chest of drawers.

That is the day my life changed—again. I've always had a different life, always. The same month my niece was going through problems in Dallas, and she called. She came too! Eating breakfast, lunch or dinner was a sanctuary in our house. At breakfast one morning I asked Curtis to watch the toast in the oven. When I came out of the bathroom, the toast was burning. Curtis was standing in front of the stove wondering what I had told him to do.

Act On It! When You See It!

Now that my brother is with me, I'll take good care of him. First we need to see the doctor because when I first saw him in Dallas, he was so thin. We see signs, but don't act on it. The doctor ruled out lots of things—came up with Alzheimer's disease. It's a degenerative brain disease of unknown cause that is the most common form of dementia and usually starts in late middle age or in old age; Curtis was 68. The results are progressive memory loss, impaired thinking, disorientation, changes in personality and mood, and degeneration of brain neurons. Act on it when you see it.

There Are Things To Laugh About!

I love theater! I used to write plays. Still do. I also have written, directed and acted. I remember Daniel Jones directed a play. I auditioned and got the part. Curtis was living with me at the time, so I had to take him everywhere I went—that included rehearsals.

I asked Curtis to sit in the audience while we rehearsed. This particular play had singing somewhere in the middle, so when we came up the stairs in rehearsal, we would start singing. It was about five or six of us coming up the stairs singing a beautiful song every night at rehearsal. Curtis learned everybody's lines, as well as, that song.

On opening night Curtis sat in his usual place, surrounded by people he had never seen before. But he was alright with that; it was rehearsal to him. When the five or six of us came up the stairs singing on opening night, and who was singing the loudest? CURTIS!

Celebrate Life

I have found so many small things to celebrate: breathing, smiling, thinking, housing, food to eat, clothes to wear, people to love, people to get upset with. Just plain old living.

Opportunities

Just the thought of celebrating is special. Celebrating life! Walking through the neighborhood and seeing a friend or meeting someone new—to share a smile. I often see people walking, pushing a grocery basket or doing something else while looking down at a cell phone. What can be so interesting that your water bottles fall from the bottom of the cart or you almost run into a little girl's foot? What could be so interesting that you can't wait until you get in the car?

Wait! I also saw a man on a motorbike talking on his cell phone. The traffic light turned green, he tried to put the phone in his pocket and almost fell. Is the cell phone that important? We have lots of opportunities to answer the phone that will not cause accidents.

Stress

"Too blessed to be stressed," is something my nephew used to say. I try not to be stressed. I really do. When people do things to hurt other people, I get a little stressed. Really, I get a lot stressed. I am learning how not to let others stress me out. When people spread gossip, WOW that's stress; I just have to tune out. The End.

The Best is Yet to Come

Can you imagine having love, joy, and peace? Try asking your body to give you all three for one whole day. Stir up that beautiful gift in you—make it real! See the gift, smell it, feel it. Remember the best is yet to come.

8 THE CABIN
Lucille Pulliam

In the summer of 1948 when I was fourteen years old my family built a small, primitive cabin in the tiny village of Allenspark in the Colorado Rocky Mountains. My mother loved the cabin and Allenspark. After my brothers and I grew up and left home, my mother spent her summers alone there until she was ninety-six years old. What follows is the story of why and how the cabin came to be, some of its history and its meaning to our family.

My father died when I was twelve years old in the spring of my seventh grade. My twin brothers, Paul and Wayne, were fifteen years old and in the ninth grade. That was in1945 before either dialysis or a kidney transplant were options for my father. So his fate was uremia and a short life.

As a young widow our mother faced several daunting challenges. First, she was now the breadwinner for our family. Because my father's death was caused by an untreatable condition, he had not been able to obtain insurance to protect his family. We did not have substantial savings, but we did have a home. Also, my mother had a college degree and had taught English in a high school briefly before her marriage. Second, Mother was now a single parent with three junior-high school age children. We were too old for day care but too young to be left unsupervised. Third, Mother was the only child of needy elderly parents. She had no sibling or cousins who could provide tangible or psychological support regarding her parents or her children.

Because Mother was determined to make a good life us, the summer after our father's death she used some of our meager savings to rent a cabin for one week in Estes Park, Colorado. She loaded Paul, Wayne and me in the family car and headed west. While in Estes Park we visited Fred and Gertrude Settles in Allenspark, which is sixteen miles south of Estes Park. Mother was acquainted with the Settles because Gertrude's brother, Lowell Bailey, was a college classmate and close friends of Mother's. Mr. Bailey was also my high school geometry teacher and driving instructor and the boys' tennis coach.

Mother was resourceful in finding sources of income. We lived in Lawrence, Kansas, a college town where housing within walking distance of the campus was in high demand. We doubled up on our own sleeping arrangements and rented rooms to college students. Mother found almost steady employment as a substitute teacher and applied for a full-time teaching position.

We returned to Colorado the next summer for another one-week vacation. My siblings and I did not realize when we made the trek to Allenspark that Mother was thinking of Allenspark as more than simply a vacation destination. That week she purchased an acre of land in the little, unincorporated town of Allenspark for $500. She arranged for Lowell Bailey to head the work crew that would build a very simple cabin on the land the following summer.

We spent a year collecting building materials for our humble abode—used windows from Sunflower Ordinance Works, used lumber from here and there, etc. We piled our motley haul onto an aged truck that my brothers drove from Lawrence all the way to Colorado. They almost didn't make it—a tire blew out landing the truck in a ditch.

Mother was resourceful and spunky. A full-time teaching position finally became available at our local high school, and it was offered to her. After negotiating the salary she said, "And I get the salary plus the $500 'head of household' bonus." The administrator, a friend and fellow church member, said, "I am sorry, Florence, women do not get a head of household bonus." My mother replied, "Who do you think is the head of our household since George died? You can look elsewhere for your English teacher. I won't be taken advantage of."

To make ends meet Mother sold our home and bought a larger

house that had been divided into four apartments. We lived in one apartment and rented the other three. By cleaning and making repairs herself Mother was soon able to save enough for the down payment on another apartment house and then another and another until she had sufficient income to support her family and help all three of us kids get college educations.

Mother's decision to not teach full time worked out great. She satisfied her love of teaching by continuing to be a substitute teacher. Being a substitute gave her the flexibility in her daily schedule she needed as a single parent and time to pursue her entrepreneurial activities that generated more income.

Mr. Bailey was a very handy guy who used his math skills to figure out how to build a cabin. My brothers and their friend Warren Robinson made up the work crew. We obtained green lumber from a nearby sawmill and obtained other supplies from Longmont and Boulder, towns located about thirty-five miles from Allenspark.

I am still in awe of Mr. Bailey who, during one of his summer breaks and with the help of three sixteen-year-old boys, was able to complete the construction of a cabin. He did it with a lot of good humor. I don't recall any complaining, but I do remember we interspersed the labor with lots of square dancing and shared meals. Mother and I fetched supplies and cooked for the crew.

My admiration for the entire cabin-building crew grew after my husband, Bill, and I became the owners of the cabin in 2001. We decided to sink a waterline underground so we could use the cabin in the winter. Our cabin sits on granite and the installer of the new pipe had to use dynamite to get below the freezing line.

The next time I talked with Wayne I asked if they had used dynamite during the original construction to set the foundation that anchors the cabin so well even seventy-one years later. Wayne said, "Oh, no! We did everything with pick and shovel. Mother wanted us to be tired at the end of the day." Hard labor was evidently one of Mother's ways of getting her three kids safely through their teenage years.

I still think fondly of Lowell Bailey—even though he asked me to quit playing tennis with Bill, my high school sweetheart and husband of sixty-five years. Mr. Bailey said I was ruining his star tennis player's game.

Paul, Wayne and I spent the summers of our high school years working in and around Allenspark. After high school our visits to the cabin were sporadic. Bill and I spent most of our working years teaching at the University of Delaware. I usually flew to Kansas at the beginning of summer in order to drive with Mother to Colorado and help her get set up to spend the summer there.

All of Mother's grandchildren spent time with her at the cabin. Two of her grandchildren even elected to have their weddings in the small picturesque church in the village. Mother missed a few summers in her cabin in order to care for her aging parents who both lived into their nineties. She tried taking them to the cabin with her, but carrying water in a ten-gallon milk can, cooking on a wood stove, and kerosene lamp for light was not to their liking. After her parents passed, Mother spent many happy summers in her cabin until she was ninety-six years old.

Mother eventually got town water, electricity and phone service. She resisted her children's attempt to install any source of heat other than the massive fireplace. She continued to carry wood to build a fire on chilly mornings and evenings.

When Mother died in 2001 at age ninety-nine-and-a-half, she left the cabin in equal shares to Paul, Wayne and me. Wayne was living in Alaska—Colorado was too tame for him—and Paul's wife could not tolerate Allenspark's 8,500-feet altitude. I could not bear to part with the cabin, so Bill and I bought my brothers' shares. By that time we had retired from our teaching positions in Delaware and moved to the Canadian Rocky Mountains in Alberta, in order to be near our older daughter who lives in Calgary. Bill was not convinced we needed a second mountain property.

Fate intervened to take us to Texas where we no longer have to shovel snow and can be near our two younger children and four grandsons. We are very grateful to be able to escape to the Colorado mountains from the Texas heat each May through September. During those months I again walk among the fragrant Ponderosa Pines—often with our grandchildren who also love to spending time in this special place.

Paul lived a few years after Bill and I became owners of the cabin. Each time we made an improvement he traveled from Kansas to celebrate the changes. His wife shared that the cabin was his favorite place on earth. Wayne, now eighty-eight years old, and his wife have left Alaska to spend their remaining years near their children in

Kansas. Each summer they come to Allenspark where Wayne delights in visiting his old haunts.

As the cabin passed from Mother to our generation, we hope we will be able to pass it on to future generations. As a reminder of our shared legacy we keep a slab of Ponderosa Pine on the front of the cabin inscribed with my mother's name and the year 1948—the year the cabin came to be.

9 ATTUNEMENT
Lucille Pulliam

There was a knock on the door. I opened it to find Nathan with his wife, Damaris, and a small, smiling, bright-eyed child. Nathan Kirkpatrick is the grandson of my girlhood friend Barbara Mitchell, who was my special friend when we were teenagers in the 1940s and 1950s and spent our summers in Allenspark.

Our family cabins were on a ridge above Skunk Hollow. Our families have kept the cabins, and Barbara and I have maintained our friendship, although at age ninety and limited by shortness of breath, Barbara no longer comes to Allenspark. Fortunately, Barbara's grandchildren and great-grandchildren still come and liven up our usually quiet ridge.

We admire how Nathan and Damaris Kirkpatrick stay trim and energetic enough to be mistaken for older siblings rather than the parents of their eight children who range in age from fourteen years to eight months. We also look forward to seeing how the interests and personalities of the children emerge and grow.

The Kirkpatricks vacation every other year in the Mitchell family cabin in Allenspark. It is expensive to fly with a family of ten, so the family travels by van from their home near Detroit, Michigan. In prior years when we answered their knock on our door we were always greeted by a group of smiling faces, but today there was only one child with the two parents.

I searched my mind to place where this winsome tyke stood in the family lineup. He must be Samuel, I decided, who was a ten-month-old babe in arms when they last visited. We invited the trio in and served them some pumpkin custard I had just removed from the oven.

Samuel sat in a rocking chair grinning as he demolished his warm custard. He delighted us with his alert and happy demeanor, but, since he did not demand attention, we were able to catch up on the Kirkpatrick family news. The two oldest Kirkpatrick children, Alexander and Eva, were now responsible teenagers capable of caring for the younger kids. This gave Nathan and Damaris the freedom to visit with only Samuel while the rest of the family stayed at their cabin.

Since their last visit to Allenspark, James, then eight months old, had joined the family. The Kirkpatrick children in order of their birth are:

Alexander, 14
Eva, 13
William, 11
Isabel, 9
Nora, 7
Providence, 5
Samuel, 3
James, 8 months

Later that day the original trio returned with the entire family. I could identify the two older children, Alexander and Eva, but the younger ones had changed so much in two years that I had difficulty identifying who was who. Isabel cheerfully corrected me when I called her Nora.

After visiting a while, Nathan invited us to their cabin for dinner, insisting they had enough spaghetti and meatballs to share. That is how I had a chance to observe this lively and harmonious clan more closely.

I prepared a salad large enough for 12 people and packed up the remaining seven portions of pumpkin custard. We drove up the hill to the Mitchell cabin with our appetites whetted for the promised spaghetti and meatballs. Alexander saw us coming and met us at the car with an offer to help carry our contributions. As we entered the cabin we were greeted by the sound of a warm, crackling fire. We admired the beauty of the fire and learned that eleven-year-old William had built it.

I handed my salad to Damaris and explained that I had kept the green onions, pumpkin seeds and kohlrabi separate in case not everyone liked them. "I give them everything, but we have never had kohlrabi. What does it taste like," Damaris asked. So I cut small slices which all of the children, except tiny James, tried. Some came back for seconds; only 3 year old Samuel spit his out.

As Damaris and Eva put the finishing touches on dinner, I chatted with Nathan. He told me they had sought and purchased their little homestead in Michigan because he and Damaris wanted the children to have chores. There was not enough for the children to do in their Michigan town. On their six acres they have a large garden and animals including fourteen sheep, three pigs, and four cats. They converted a small Model T garage into a sugar house for processing maple syrup which they obtain from a neighbor's trees.

After dinner the three older children—Alexander, Eva and William—and the adults played *Estimate*, a card game we traditionally play in our little community. The three younger girls washed the dishes and then played contently with each other and Samuel. Baby James sat placidly in a high chair at our table.

The following are things that I learned from observing and talking with the children that evening:

All of the children were invested in and proud of doing their assigned job. Alexander, 14, exuded competence and confidence. He took care of the pigs.

Eva, who just turned thirteen, was transiting from childhood to womanhood. At home in Michigan she took care of the sheep. Eva had made some amazing observations during and after the ewes' lambing, including stillbirths—things that are not included in the curriculum of city kids. She also adopted a raccoon that became a family pet and followed two-year-old Samuel around.

William, who celebrated his eleventh birthday on the trip, looked remarkably like a younger version of his dad, down to the sandy hair with cowlick. William chopped and carried the wood and built and tended the fires.

That evening I did not have a chance to talk with the younger girls, but these were some of my impressions from observing them:

Isabel, nine, stood out because of her darker hair and air of independence.

Nora, age seven, was sporting a cute, blond bob. She was very affectionate, especially toward Samuel, giving him squeezes and kisses.

Providence, age five, blended with the group, but her parents said she was a non-conformist.

We finished our game of *Estimate*, bid everyone goodnight and returned to our cabin.

The next day I stopped by the Mitchell cabin and asked if anyone cared to walk to the post office with me. To my delight, everyone said they would come—except Nathan and Alexander who were away getting parts for car repair. This walk gave me a chance to test some of my impressions of the children with Damaris.

Yes, **Isabel** is independent and has been from birth. "In fact," Damaris confided, "she is so independent that she has hardly needed me. For example, once she was hurt and instead of coming to me for help she simply went to the bathroom, cleaned herself up and took care of her own wounds. It has sometimes made me feel bad that she didn't need me because I feel I don't know her as well as I know my other children."

Regarding **Nora** she told me, "She has been my biggest challenge. She was super fussy from birth. I finally figured out that she needed more physical contact than the others and that has made all the difference." During our spaghetti and meatballs dinner Nora sat next to her mother, and I observed lots of good eye contact between them. Although I had seen both parents giving attention to all the children with no evidence of favoritism, I thought perhaps there was a special bond between this mother and daughter, as there is sometimes between people who are on the same wavelength. Damaris, however, believes she has special bonds with all of her children and is simply responding to Nora's unique needs.

Providence, the "non-conformist," is a huggable preschooler with a winning smile. Her mother told me she has been slower to grow out of a whining stage that all children seem to go through between two and four. My guess is that Providence is trying to discover and express her unique talents and make her contributions.

I asked Damaris about her children's academic and intellectual development. Damaris homeschools her children which gives her many opportunities to observe their growth on many levels.

Bill and I marveled at the harmony and good feeling we sensed during our time with this family. How do they have the wisdom and energy to avoid conflict and function consistently with apparent love and good will? The word ATTUNEMENT came to mind. I looked up the definition of attunement and found: "Attunement is the practice of opening thought and feeling to the source of wisdom and love which is within all people. It is the shared generation of life energy promoting health and wellbeing and is a daily practice."

Don't you think the world would be a better place if we all learned to practice attunement at an early age?

10 STORIES
Sharon Vasquez

Bullies

At the ripe young age of sixty-five I was bullied. I remember as a child growing up there was a girl that rode the same school bus as me. She always tried to pick fights. She looked for anything and anyway to cause a problem. I always stayed close to my friend Moses who lived across the street from me. Moses played on the basketball team. He was tall and looked so much older than me; he was my source of personal protection then.

But now at sixty-five I had to protect myself, and I thought truth was the answer. I used my pen to write of the awful abusive threats, the vulgar language and lack of professionalism I experienced. I tried to hide my fears, keep a stiff upper lip and rise above it. Yet anger grew inside me.

The anger came from my disappointment with myself. The feeling that I had no choice but to take the bullying wore on me. I wanted to be heard, but my tormentor was evil and had poisoned the water against me.

Good can conquer evil. Truth is simply truth. By the time we are seniors we have already gone through hard knocks and gained much wisdom. I have personally grown from my life experiences and still hope to learn every day from others. My fight is not over, and I hope if you are bullied you find the strength to stand up for yourself.

Grandma Rose

My step-grandmother's name was Rose. She was a lovely Italian woman who married my paternal grandfather when I was young. It was hard for me to explain that I had three grandmothers, but it never really never mattered.

We always looked forward to going to Grandma Rose's house because we would eat the best spaghetti and meatballs ever. She also had star bread from the Italian bakery, and, yes, it looked like a star with five points. She always served buffet style, and we would walk around the dining room table and fill our plates with pasta, sauce and meatballs. Our portions were always more than we should eat but our delight from the taste of the food was worth an extra full tummy.

On one of Grandma Rose's cabinets sat two off-white figurines of a sitting boy and girl in vintage clothing. I always told Grandma Rose how much I liked the statues and thought they were beautiful. I now own three sets of the boy and girl figurines and one of them is the set I admired as a young girl.

Grandpa
I will always remember Grandpa bouncing me on his knee. I don't know at what age it started, but I remember when it stopped. My grandpa was an immigrant from Poland and was imprisoned in a camp. He never spoke of it, and he wore only long-sleeve shirts. He was kind and gentle and smoked cigars. My grandma made him sit by a filter system so the smell from the cigar would not go into the house, and he could never smoke when we were there. It didn't mean that he could not have that cigar in his mouth. He would call me his little "poohpa leaneee." I never knew what it meant, but I always laughed with joy.

Where did your name come from?
When I found out I was having a baby it was a time of joy for the future and sadness for the past. My grandpa had gone to heaven, and I was in shock because he passed away on Sunday morning after retiring on Friday. My doctor was not sure I should go to his funeral, but I had to be there to say good-bye.

While sitting in the service with such heavy sorrow I made a big decision, one that would carry on his name forever. I decided, whether I had a boy or girl, the child would be his namesake. When I had my baby the doctor held up the baby's back side to me and said,

"Guess what you had." I said, "A healthy baby." He said, "Yes, and it's a girl." So, my daughter's name is Stephanie, after her great-grandfather Stephen, as well as her grandfather Stephen.

Eating at Grandma B.'s house

My parents and grandparents lived through the Great Depression. This was a time when they had little to eat. Maybe this is why Grandma B. was always concerned about us going hungry. Every time we saw her she always made sure we took food home with us. The conversation usually started with, "Are you hungry?" My usual response was, "Not yet Grandma." Then it was, "Do you want a sandwich?" I would respond, "No." Then she would say, "Do you want mustard and mayonnaise on it," and I'd say, "No," and *presto magico* there sat a sandwich on the table for me. That was just an appetizer. Next came the huge pot of cabbage rolls. They were so good, but, even after we were stuffed, she would continue to force feed us. After all of that there was desert, and she would use whatever she had to make us a great treat. On one occasion she made cake inside of ice cream cones then frosted them; it was shocking but delightful. She always liked to experiment with foods and flavors.

Dying with Dignity

Living in a senior community we see the passing of many souls. There is one person in particular that touched my heart in so many ways. For the sake of this story I will call her Angel. Angel was very devoted to her family, church and friends. She served with pleasure to walk among us with grace. She became ill but embraced every ounce of life she had in her. I was fortunate to spend her last birthday with her and her family. We talked about dying, and I told her I was not ready yet. She looked a bit disappointed at me and said, "We all are dying." In closing, she died her way by setting a path for her family and friends to follow, by having a master plan for her life's ending, leaving nothing behind but blessings.

The Truck Fire

Moving is daunting, but to move across the country is harder. Traveling down the road with our most valued possessions was even scarier when our rental truck caught on fire half way to our destination. It happened. We watched all the cherished memories we thought too valuable to let the movers take, go up in flames. The firemen who came to our rescue picked up the few pieces of our life that were not gone and handed them to us and apologized for nothing that was in their control. Sometimes you think life is too much to bear. You are kneeling on the gravel crying for your loss until you come to your senses and realize you have lost things, not people, and your loved one is right beside you. Reality.

Friends & Family

You do not have to born into a family to be family. I have many lifelong friends I met later in life. These friends are men and women of every nationality. I came from a military family, and we traveled all the time. I lived an ever-changing life and never saw or looked for the differences in people. Friends can become family easily as our lives change and as we share experiences that build upon our relationship. When you have a true friend, you can be yourself always and say whatever you need to say. It feels like wearing a comfortable pair of slippers. Being accepting of each other with open hearts and minds is how our lives grow.

Love

What is love? I hear people talk about loving a dress, a meal, a movie or a person, but are these things in the same category? My thought is "no," so I try to use the word "love" for people only. Why? It is because when I say, "I love you," I want it to mean something more than a passing thought. I want to express a feeling between one heart and another. I want my words to stand for something that is forever, that makes you feel special, touches you inside and lets you know it's always and forever, unwavering and solid. When I tell my grandson how much I love him, I hope one day he sees what I mean by that: I will be forever there for you, through thick and thin, no matter what. No Matter What.

The Raffle

I met my husband in Las Vegas. I worked for an office furniture and supply company that did business with a major chair company. I was invited to attend an opening of a new warehouse which sold their products. At the door I was handed a raffle ticket for a free trip to the company's annual convention in Las Vegas, all expenses paid. I happily filled out the ticket and threw it into the box.

Tom, the national sales manager for the chair company, called out to everyone to please be quiet when it was time to pick the raffle ticket for the trip. Tom asked a young child to pull one raffle ticket from the box. He looked at it and read my name. I was shocked and delighted; I was a 25-year-old woman, and this would be my first trip by myself. I was ready for the experience.

The convention was held at The Riviera. Sadly, it has been knocked down, but forty years ago I was there. I had traveled from Dallas to Las Vegas wide-eyed and not knowing what to expect. The first night the chair company sponsored a cocktail party. I knew no one and felt awkward. Then I saw Tom, the national sales manager. I approached him, we made some small talk and I said, "Who are the single men here?" Tom's eyes opened wide, and I thought I had said something wrong. He said, "Wait right here. I have someone I want you to meet."

I stood in terror of what I had said and wondered who he wanted me to meet. What had I done? Within a few minutes Tom returned with a skinny man who had long hair and hippie beads around his neck. I wanted to run, but there was something about his goofy smile that I found attractive.

The cocktail party attendees were ushered into another room for a dinner show. The skinny guy—his name was Ed—stayed by my side. I felt safe. I could excuse myself at any time, right? Well, I cannot tell you what I ate, but I'm sure it wasn't much; I found Ed fascinating, and he kept holding my hand! His laugh was honest and sincere, and since we were seated with others the pressure was off. Joan Rivers performed, and she was unusual but entertaining. At the end of the show Ed asked me if I wanted to walk down The Strip. I said sure, so we walked hand in hand to several casinos and he bought me nickels for the slots. At that time Las Vegas kept the drinks flowing as long as you were spending money. I really wasn't much of a drinker so water worked for me.

Time flew by that evening. I couldn't put a finger on it, but there was something amazing about this kind, sweet, honest and gentle man. It was the in the early morning hours that we strolled back to our hotel. As we walked by The Wedding Chapel I turned to Ed and said, "You are going to marry me. Let's do it now, or it will cost more later." He laughed and said sure, but we kept walking.

The next night I told my mother over the phone I had met the man I thought I would marry. She thought I had been drinking too much or was drugged and wanted me to come home. At just about that time Ed came to pick me up for dinner. I handed him the phone and said, "My mom wants to talk to you." His eyes opened wide as I pushed the phone towards him. He stumbled and laughed a bit as he talked, and soon they hung up.

We went to dinner at a Mexican restaurant and then to the old downtown via a city bus. I had never been on a city bus. It was a great night. I remember looking at him and feeling more and more attracted to him. I wish I could explain how I felt, but it was such a different feeling. I was in love. No! How could I love someone I hardly knew? What was wrong with me?

The next day Ed had to go home. I went to the front door of the hotel to see him off. I had one more day in Vegas. I stood there with him as a limo arrived to pick him up. The driver loaded his luggage. Ed handed me his business card. Then he kissed me good-bye.

After Ed left I was devastated. Almost my entire time in Vegas we were together, and he had just left with not much to say. I felt naïve, a dumb, little girl with feelings for someone I had just met. I moped around the Riviera, packed for my flight the next day and tried not to think about that guy.

I returned to work on Monday. As I walked towards my desk, I could hear my phone ringing. I had arrived early that morning, and the phone was already ringing! I picked it up and heard a familiar voice say, "You didn't tell me your phone number was unlisted," and my reply was "You never asked."

Ed had called me at work; it seems he did care for me after all. By noon I had a dozen red roses, and within two months we were married. I'm proud to say we have been through just about everything together, and we are still strong at forty years of marriage. It was the luck of the draw. I met my husband, because I won a raffle. We are blessed.

11 GRANDMOTHERS
Paula Alvelo

One of my grandmothers was hard to please and did nothing but sit inside her house with the blinds closed. I didn't like spending time with her. Wouldn't you know that we got stuck living with her for a couple of years when I was a little girl?

My other grandmother was the opposite: always smiling and glad to see me. She made her own yeast rolls, which to this day I can smell. Everything she cooked was delicious, and she specialized in Italian food. I told my mother that even her saltine crackers tasted better than the ones we had at home.

This fun grandmother had a huge vegetable garden bordered by giant flowers like gladioli and hydrangeas. She introduced me to zucchini, which I loved. Years later, when she told me zucchini was really a squash, I felt a tad betrayed. She knew I would never have eaten squash on purpose.

12 MARRIAGE PROPOSAL
Jeanetta Doan

This story takes place in the middle to latter part of the 1800s in Brownsville, Texas. It is the story of Tomasa Conde Saldana. Tomasa was dating a young man, and her beau wanted to marry her. She was in agreement, but before she could give consent he had to ask her father for permission as this was the custom in those times.

The young man went to Tomasa's father—my great-grandfather—and asked for Tomasa's hand in marriage. My great-grandfather insisted the suitor answer a question correctly. This was the question: "If you and Tomasa had only one egg between you, what would you do with it?" The young man answered, "Of course I would give half to Tomasa, and keep half for myself." My great-grandfather answered, "That is not the correct answer." Tomasa's beau was confused. "What is the correct answer," he asked. "The correct answer is that you should give the whole egg to my daughter," my great-grandfather said.

That's right! My Great-Aunt Tomasa never married and became a bitter old maid.

13 THE FOUR-POSTER BED
Jeanetta Doan

This story takes place during the time of Pancho Villa between Matamoros, Mexico, and Brownsville, Texas. My great-grandmother Romona Conde de Saldana had two ranches. One in Brownsville, the other in Matamoros. Pancho liked to visit my great-grandmother. On one occasion he sent a scout to her ranch in Matamoros to let her know that he—and his army—would be coming. That meant she was expected to feed them all..

The preparation began. Tamales were made, beans were cooked, tortillas were made and the fattened calf was slaughtered. Along with the preparing of food Romona found time to make other preparations for Pancho's arrival—protecting her personal property and treasures.

Romona had the columns of her four-poster bed sawed in half and hollowed out. In those spaces she hid her money and jewelry. When the bed was put back together Pancho was none the wiser.

14 VIETNAM
Mel Garza

When this picture taken I (left) was training prior to being deployed to Vietnam in 1969. I commanded a PBR (Patrol Boat, River) during my year in Vietnam and made over one hundred combat patrols. I was involved in several fire fights and was awarded the Bronze Star with Valor and several other awards for service. I retired from the Navy in 1973, after serving with pride and honor for twenty-five years.

ABOUT THE AUTHORS

The authors of this work are a community of storytellers in Austin, Texas, though few are native Texans. They remember fondly stories passed down by their elders—stories of lakes and ponds and mountains and beaches and sandy creek beds. The authors wish to share their stories so they may not be lost and may bring joy to others.